3 IN 1: THE CHARACTER OF GOD

3 IN 1: THE CHARACTER OF GOD

by
Stephen Baker

RITCHIE
John Ritchie Publishing

40 Beansburn, Kilmarnock, Scotland

ISBN-13: 978 1 914273 43 8

Scripture quotations in this book are taken from the New King James Version (NKJV) unless noted otherwise, for example, AV (the Authorised or King James Version) or ESV (the English Standard Version).

Typeset by John Ritchie Ltd., Kilmarnock
Printed by Bell & Bain Ltd., Glasgow

Contents

INTRODUCTION

The question, 'What is God like?', is always one that will provoke discussion and debate. To get an answer, there are two possible approaches.

1. The best scenario would be for God to tell us what He is like. That would save a lot of conjecture and give us an accurate answer.

2. We could use the evidence we have available to establish that God exists, and then try to ascertain what type of being He is, how He thinks, and how He operates.

This second approach has severe limitations as we are restricted by the sum total of human experience (assuming that it has been recorded and retained accurately). Also, our results will be very subjective as we will end up describing God in terms that we have chosen. They may not be accurate. This could ultimately be defined as personal speculation.

I suggest that the first approach is available to us in the holy book we call the Bible. We are not left to our own personal speculations about God, for we can learn from the revelation which God has given about Himself in His book.

It is, therefore, important for us to consider why we should accept that the Bible is in reality God's message to the human race, and that it has supernatural authorship. If it is just another 'holy book' written by men, then it is only another form of speculation.

This will be the subject of Chapter 1 which I hope you will read carefully.

CHAPTER 1

Verifying the Bible as God's Word

As a Christian, I am totally convinced that the Bible is more than just the writings of men. The Bible is actually a library of 66 books, and we believe that this ancient collection of books was written by men, but that they were not the source of the information.

Peter, a disciple of Jesus, wrote, 'Prophecy never came by the will of man, but holy men of God spoke as they were moved by the Holy Spirit' (2 Peter 1.21). Somehow God allowed men to write in their own style (you can distinguish John's writings from Paul's and so on), but what they wrote was not the result of their own research or an expression of their own ideas. For instance, Peter states, in the same chapter referred to above, 'Knowing this first, that no prophecy of Scripture is of any private interpretation'. This means that the prophets did not invent their own prophecies (v.20), for their impulse for prophesying came from God (v.21).[1]

Over 3,000 times, the writers of the Bible claim to be speaking for God. Therefore, the claim that God is the author of Bible is implied repeatedly. But the Bible also makes this claim explicitly over and over again. Let me give you a few sample Scriptures.

---

[1] 2 Peter 1:21 - Eyewitnesses of His Majesty - Bible Hub. https://biblehub.com/2_peter/1-21.htm

1. In Exodus chapter 31 verse 18, Moses claims that God personally wrote the 10 commandments.

2. The apostle Paul claims, in 2 Timothy chapter 3 verse 16, that all Scripture is inspired by God and it is good for those who read and obey it.

3. In 2 Peter chapter 1 verses 20 and 21, Peter states that the prophets did not make the Bible up.

4. In John chapter 10 verse 35, the Lord Jesus states that the truth of Scripture cannot be broken.

5. The prophet Isaiah writes, in chapter 66 verse 1, that his message is directly from God (all of the prophets make this claim).

6. In Matthew chapter 5 verse 18, the Lord Jesus states that every detail of Scripture will be fulfilled before this universe ceases to exist. He believed that the Old Testament Scriptures were the Word of God and He predicted that the New Testament Scriptures would be written. In fact, the Lord Jesus Christ claimed that the Bible was God's Word and He staked His reputation on that claim. So either He is God and His Word is flawless or both Christ and His Word are false.[2]

These, of course, are all claims that the Bible makes for itself. That in itself doesn't mean the claims are true. So how can we be sure? We need to be sure that the Bible is genuine if we are going to believe what it teaches about the character of God - indeed

---

[2]Claims of Divine Authorship | Answers in Genesis. https://answersingenesis.org/the-word-of-god/2-claims-of-divine-authorship/

if we are going accept anything it states as truth, including our need of salvation, forgiveness and the grace of God. While this is not the main purpose of this book, being able to verify the Bible as the unique communication from our Creator is vital before we consider what it teaches about the Godhead and the Trinity.

Scripture has been written so that we can verify its truthfulness in those areas that we understand and can check out. There are many such areas, but here are four examples:

1. History - all archeological research to date has demonstrated the accuracy of the Bible.

2. Scientific accuracy - all proven scientific and medical developments are in agreement with what the Bible teaches in these areas.

3. Unity - the Bible has unity of thought and truth from beginning to end. It has a consistent presentation of truth and ethics from Genesis to Revelation.

4. Prophecy - predicting the future is a risky business. People who made inaccurate and intentionally false predictions in the days of the Bible were prosecuted and executed for claiming, falsely, to speak for God. All the Bible's predictions that have been fulfilled to date have been accurate. A selection of these is found in the book of Daniel and they involve the nation of Israel. Predictions about the birth, life, death and resurrection of Jesus Christ are prolific, and are staggering in their accuracy.

If the Bible is demonstrably accurate about these things that we do understand, it should give us the confidence to believe what it says about things that we have no knowledge of, i.e., God, the origin of life, consciousness, the future, the unseen world, etc.

It is an amazing fact that the Bible made statements about things that men at the time of writing had no way of knowing, and scientific research and development has since proved them to be true.

I hope that I have at least shown you some ways in which the Bible can be proven to be the Word of God and, therefore, worthy of your trust. My point here is that because the Bible is accurate in the areas of life we are able to check out then it is reasonable to rely on its truthfulness when it speaks about matters of our origin and spiritual matters that we are not in a position to verify. Ultimately, the truth about salvation and our relationship with God is something that has to be experienced as well as discussed.

Many excellent books have been written demonstrating in detail that the Bible is the Word of God. A list of these books is given at the end of this short book.

So, let's get back to what the Bible says about the character and personality of God, but before I start here is a little piece of advice and a warning.

A little piece of advice and a warning

Please do not believe anything I write in this book if you cannot find a reference to support it in the Bible. The Bible itself is the final and authoritative source of truth concerning God, His character and His world.

In light of this advice, you are going to have to work with me to get the best value out of this book. I am going to refer you to lots of Scriptures: please look up the references and take time to think about each verse. This might be hard work at times, but it is the only way to understand the truth of Scripture. I might refer to verses more than once in different chapters, but this is because I am making a different point on each occasion.

My prayer is that this book will cause you love, worship and obey the Father, Son, and Holy Spirit, and that it will all be for the glory of God.

CHAPTER 2

The Trinity and the Character and Personality of God

Before we explore what the Bible says about God, I must remind you that just because we find something hard to understand or we feel that it is outside of our area of expertise, this does not mean that it is not true.

Often people will not accept what is clearly stated in Scripture, because they have already decided what they believe. The tendency for all of us is to read everything in light of our own fixed ideas. The challenge is to read Scripture with an open mind and to accept its teaching at face value.

These principles are vitally important when it comes to considering truth about God.

Here are some general characteristics of God. He is:
- All-knowing
- Unlimited geographically
- Timeless and eternal
- All-powerful, no limit to His power
- Sovereign, unrestricted and unguided (apart from being guided by His moral perfection) in how He chooses to act.

I will talk about these characteristics of God (and some more) in greater detail in another chapter when we discuss whether the Father, the Son and the Spirit all have the same key qualities.

Now, let's consider what Christians mean when they talk about **The Trinity**. Simply put, they are stating that they believe that the Bible teaches that God is one Being composed of three distinct Persons. This will be a strange concept to you if it is the first time that you have considered it.

Some people will say to you that the Bible never uses the word *trinity*. They are correct. It doesn't use the actual word *trinity*, but the truth of the Trinity is in the Bible, and the word has been used to describe accurately God's personhood.

The word *trinity* is a combination of two words, *tri-*, meaning three, and *unity*, meaning one. *Trinity* means three-in-one, or one-in-three. The Bible does not teach, and Christians do not believe, that there are three gods. They believe that there is one God (one Being), but that He is composed of three Persons – the Father, the Son, and the Holy Spirit. Nor do Christians believe merely that this one God reveals Himself in three different ways, such as when one man may be a husband, a father, and a son. No, the Bible teaches that God is one Being, but that He exists in, or is composed of, three Persons. He is a *Tripartite Being*. He is complex, holy and supreme, and beyond human imagination and reasoning. So, we can't expect to fully understand Him, just as an insect or fish doesn't understand or relate to humans. We are different beings, living in different spheres.

At a very basic level, the very fact that God loves, demands that He is a Being made up of more than one Person. Love can only be expressed when there is someone to love. Who did God love before the creation of people or angelic spirit beings? The answer is love was expressed between the three members of the Godhead. The Father loved the Son, the Son loved the Spirit, the Spirit loved the Father, the Son loved the Father, and so on. You can also apply this to other characteristics of God.

One amazing revelation in Scripture is that God made humans in His image (Genesis 1.26-31). We were created to be like God. We were made to represent God and to reflect His character and moral values. It is wonderful that God has revealed Himself to us through His Word (the Bible) and ultimately through His Son becoming a man. The incarnation (God becoming man) is another clear evidence that humans are a distinct type of being. We were created to be like God but are essentially different. If this were not the case, the Lord Jesus would never have had to become a man. Through the incarnation of the Son of God it is possible for humans to have a relationship with God.

Augustine, a theologian who lived 354 - 430 AD, once wrote a book on the Trinity. He said this about the Trinity, 'If you don't believe in the Trinity, you will lose your soul. But if you try to understand it, you will lose your mind'.

CHAPTER 3

What does the Old Testament say about the Trinity?

Many, if not all, Bible writers made reference to the three persons of the Godhead as they wrote Scripture.

Throughout the rest of this book you will find references where God the Father, the Son, and the Holy Spirit are mentioned in the same section. You should read them all carefully and consider what they teach. I am going to select some of them to explain how they have convinced me that God is unique, in that He is one God and yet the three Persons of the Father, Son, and Holy Spirit.

Genesis 1.1

The very first verse of the Bible has hidden within it the truth about the personhood of God. Hebrew words can be singular, dual, or plural. Singular is obvious, dual is two and plural is three or more. The Newberry Bible has very useful tools to help people, who have no knowledge of Hebrew, to identify what number each word has. For instance, in Genesis chapter 1 verse 1, the word for God is plural, meaning that God is made of three or more. If you were reading and understanding a Hebrew Bible for the first time, you might be puzzled to find out that God is 'three or more', but you wouldn't really know the significance of this fact at this stage.

Genesis 1.26

In this verse we are allowed to listen in to a conversation between the members of the Godhead: God said, '*Let Us* make man in *Our* image, according to *Our* likeness; let them have dominion over the fish of the sea, over the birds of the air, and over the cattle, over all the earth and over every creeping thing that creeps on the earth'. It reads so simply. We would have no insight into the way God thinks without passages like these. But how can a conversation take place if there is no one to talk to? So, note the words - 'God said, "Let *Us* make man in *Our* image, according to *Our* likeness."' It seems quite simple to me. At least two members of the Godhead are speaking, and from the first verse of the chapter, we know that there are at least three.

Genesis 3.22

The final reference in these early chapters of Genesis is in chapter 3. As before, we are listening in to a conversation between the members of the Godhead. God says, 'Behold, the man is become as one of *us*' [AV]. Look carefully and honestly. What else can the passage mean? This booklet is not the place to discuss the implications of sin entering the world. The reason I selected the passage is that it clearly records one member of the Godhead talking to another member.

Frederick Faber, an English hymn writer, summarised it well when he wrote:

> *Timeless, spaceless, single, lonely,*
> *Yet sublimely Three,*
> *Thou art grandly, always, only*
> *God in unity.*

It has been pointed out that the word 'lonely' in this poem doesn't mean that God needed friends, but it is the idea that God is a solitary being. One of the features of the Trinity is that God is self-sufficient in Himself, He is contented socially and, therefore, satisfied with the company of the Father, Son, and Spirit. This does, however, make all the more wonderful and generous the grace of God in seeking the company of humans.

The next reference I want you to look at is found in Deuteronomy chapter 6 verses 4-5. Moses recorded in writing the law that God gave to him on Mount Sinai. Deuteronomy is the second record of the giving of the law. In chapter 6 Moses is explaining why the law was given:

1. The people had to be taught to obey the law.
2. The land God had given them had to be occupied in a way that glorified God.
3. It was for God's chosen people, Israel.
4. It was for their good.
5. It was so that they would grow as a nation.

(The only way we can grow spiritually is when we obey, do, and benefit from the Word of God.)

These points are covered in the first three verses of Deuteronomy chapter 6. In verse 4, Moses appeals to his fellow countrymen by reminding them, 'The LORD our God, the LORD is one'. He wants the Israelites to love their God (v.5), to store His commandments in their heart (v.6), and to teach their children the same thing (v.7-15).

The point of referring to this passage is to note the use of the expression 'is one'. This is very interesting as it is the same word that is used in Genesis chapter 2 verse 24 when talking about a man leaving his father and his mother, cleaving to his wife and becoming *'one flesh'*. Two people are described as one flesh as a result of marriage. Is this significant? I think it is and this helps me understand how God who is one LORD can be made up of three persons, the Father, the Son, and the Holy Spirit. The clear understanding that this is the case is not fully explained until you come to the New Testament, but the seed of the idea is seen in these Old Testament Scriptures. There are more - let us look at some of them.

Psalm 2

Psalm 2 is a striking example of a conversation between members of the Godhead in heaven. The Psalm projects our minds to a day when the rulers, people and nations of the world will be obliged to acknowledge the Father and the Son and to take the advice of the Holy Spirit.

The Psalm divides very naturally into four main sections. The first section (verses 1-3) sets the scene - the world and its leaders are rebelling against God. Even in that section we see the Father and the Son are mentioned as different people. In verse 2 we read, 'The kings of the earth set themselves, and the rulers take counsel together, against the LORD and against His Anointed [Christ]'.

Before Jesus returns to earth, the Bible predicts that the leaders of the earth will rebel against God; you will read about this in many Bible books - Daniel 2, 7, Zechariah 12-14, Matthew 24, Luke 21, 2 Thessalonians 2, Revelation 13, etc.

The noteworthy thing in Psalm 2 is that God is described as (1) the LORD, and (2) His Anointed. Taking into account other Scriptures, we now know that this is referring to the Father and the Lord Jesus.

The following three sections of Psalm 2 all record the words of the Father, the Son, and the Holy Spirit.

Verses 4-6: The Father

> Note who is speaking: He, the Lord.
> What does He say?
> 'Yet I have set My King on My holy hill of Zion' (v 6).

The Father is announcing that He will crown His King in Zion, which is His ancient centre of power in Jerusalem.

Verses 7-9: The Son

The language then changes. It cannot be the Father speaking as it is a response to the previous statement. 'The LORD has said to Me, "You are My Son, today I have begotten You"' (v 7).

The Son tells us what the Father said to Him. This is an eternal statement which we as humans find hard to understand. There was never a point when the eternal Father had or obtained an eternal Son. The term 'begotten' describes a relationship. The term 'this day' does not describe a point in time when the Son of God became the Son. God is timeless and so is His Son. Every time this expression is mentioned in the Bible, it confirms the relationship that the Lord Jesus *always* had with the Father as the Son of God. It is used in Acts 13 verses 33 and 34 at the resurrection of the Lord Jesus, and in Hebrews 1 verse 5 when the Lord Jesus went back to heaven to be glorified and when it is predicted that the Lord Jesus will come again to this planet in majesty and glory.

In verses 8 and 9 the Father replies to the Son, 'Ask of Me, and I will ...'

Verses 10-12: The Holy Spirit.

In this final section of the Psalm, the Holy Spirit speaks. He talks about what the Father has said: verse 10, 'Be wise ... Be instructed'. He gives advice: verse 11, 'Serve the Lord with fear, and rejoice with trembling'.

Then the Spirit of God gives advice about the Son of God: verse 12, 'Kiss the Son, lest He be angry ... Blessed are all those who put their trust in Him'.

These passages need to be read and thought about carefully, but I think an honest reading of them (in the light of other Scriptures) makes it clear that more than one person of the Godhead is speaking.

Psalm 110

Verse 1: 'The LORD said to my Lord, "Sit at My right hand ..."'
In Matthew chapter 22 verses 41 to 46, the Lord Jesus makes it very clear that this ancient passage was about Him.

Isaiah 6.3, 8

This is a wonderful passage where Isaiah describes a vision that he had. It happened to Isaiah in the same year that the King Uzziah died. He had a vision of God on His throne in heaven, just when an earthly king had vacated his throne. The lesson - I think he is reminding us that God is still in control even if events on earth seem to be rapidly changing.

Many Old Testament prophets were staggered when God appeared to them. This one was no exception. Isaiah describes the scene in graphic detail. My reason for looking at this passage is that it is an example of another conversation that takes place in heaven. Verse 8 records this. Isaiah 'heard the voice of the Lord, saying, "Whom shall I send, and who will go for Us?"'

It is hard to ignore the word 'Us'. Who is speaking? – the Lord (v.8). In the same sentence, the Lord speaks as one person - 'Whom shall I send', and as more than one - 'Who shall go for *Us*'. Interesting! I think it supports the case that I am making.

Isaiah 7.14

A prediction is made about a child being born of a virgin. This was fulfilled in the birth of Jesus. Matthew chapter 1 verse 23 confirms that this refers to the Lord Jesus, and that one of His names would be Immanuel, which means 'God with us'. This presents to us two members of the Godhead.

In Isaiah chapter 9 verses 6 and 7, we have a clear prediction of a child to be born and a son who would be given. The same person would be God on earth (Mighty God, Everlasting Father). These verses highlight the fact that the man who is known as Jesus is also the one who is referred to as God.

In Isaiah chapter 40 verse 9 and chapter 52 verse 7, there are clear Messianic predictions which the New Testament claims to be about the Lord Jesus. These references are fulfilled in the preaching of John the Baptist as he announced the coming of Messiah, Jesus. See Matthew chapter 3, Mark chapter 1, Luke chapter 3, and John chapter 1.

So now we have looked at some verses from the Old Testament that indicate that God is a trinity. These sample verses have been taken from the three main sections of the Old Testament: the Law, the Psalms, and the Prophets.

CHAPTER 4

What does the New Testament say about the Trinity?

The Old Testament was first translated into Greek around 250 BC. At this stage, the name 'Jehovah' or *Yahweh* was translated as *Kurios*, i.e., 'the Lord'. This translation then influenced how the New Testament was written. In the New Testament, we get a more precise definition of the expression, 'the LORD'. The amazing claim of the New Testament is that Jesus is 'the LORD' of whom we read in the Old Testament.

Saying, 'Jesus is Lord', became the key test of Christian authenticity, see 1 Corinthians 12.3. The New Testament also claims that the Holy Spirit is Lord: 'Now the Lord is that Spirit; and where the Spirit of the Lord is, there is liberty' (2 Corinthians 3.17).

> So, God the Father is Lord.
> God the Son is Lord.
> God the Holy Spirit is Lord.

But Ephesians chapter 4 verse 5 and 6 states there is only one Lord: 'One Lord ... one God'.

God is Lord, but made up of three persons, as we have been discovering in the Old Testament.

The New Testament explanation of the term 'the Lord' helps us explain the Old Testament use of term 'the LORD'. The seed of the truth of the Trinity is sown in the Old Testament and is then expanded upon in the New Testament.

Here is another verse from the New Testament that states this truth clearly: 'Yet for us there is one God, the Father, of whom are all things, and we for Him; and one Lord Jesus Christ, through whom are all things, and through whom we live' (1 Corinthians 8.6). We, as Christians, confess the truth of the Trinity on the basis of Holy Scripture.

- The Bible teaches a Triune Creator: Genesis 1.1, 2, Psalm 33.6, John 1.1–3, and the truth of a Triune Redeemer in Galatians chapter 4 verses 4–6.

- The New Testament teaches us to be baptised in God's Triune name, Matthew 28.19, and calls us to bless God's Triune name for all the spiritual blessings we have through the work of the Father, the Son, and the Holy Spirit (Ephesians 1.3–14).

- God also blesses us in His Triune name in 2 Corinthians chapter 13 verse 14: 'The grace of the Lord Jesus Christ and the love of God and the fellowship of the Holy Spirit be with you all' [ESV].

Now look at some additional verses from the Gospel records.

Matthew 3.16, 17

The Lord Jesus is being baptised in the River Jordan. The Holy Spirit comes down from heaven to the Lord Jesus (notice the Holy Spirit is called the Spirit of God, verse 16). There is a voice from heaven (the Father says, 'This is My beloved Son'). So in this passage there are three distinct persons and all three are described as God in various ways. The same event is described by John in the first chapter of his Gospel. In verse 34, John the Baptist calls the Lord Jesus, 'the Son of God'. I think that all would accept that the voice from heaven was the voice of God, and at this stage God calls the Lord Jesus His 'beloved Son', Matthew 3.17.

There is great significance in what God the Father says on this occasion. He pays the Lord Jesus an incredibly high compliment by not only announcing that He is His Son, but also that He is greatly loved. He stresses that He, the Father, gets great joy from the Son. All of these statements added together have outstanding implications. There are no records of any other man being given that level of accolade from God. In Isaiah, we read twice (42.8, 48.11) that God will not give His glory to anyone else, but here He is glorifying the Son. Even in this we see the inference that God is sharing His glory with One who is His equal (John 17.1, 5).

So, when I compare all four passages (Matthew 3.13-17, Mark 1.9-11, Luke 3.21-22, John 1.29-34), and read the description of the baptism of the Lord Jesus, I come away convinced that all the members of the Godhead were involved in that baptism.

In Isaiah 40 verse 9, a prediction is made about the coming of the Lord Jesus to Jerusalem and the people of Judah. With the benefit of hindsight, we can now see that this Scripture was foretelling the coming of Messiah to the nation of Israel. The early church and the writers of the New Testament believed this to be the case as they applied it to the Lord Jesus, in Matthew 3.1-3, Mark 1.1-8, Luke 3.1-9, 15-17 and John 1.19-29. Notice that Isaiah says, 'Prepare the way of the LORD; make straight in the desert a highway for our God' (v.3), but the Gospel writers say, 'Prepare the way of the LORD', applying it to the Lord Jesus. It is clear from these two passages that the Lord Jesus is Lord and God.

Luke chapter 8 verse 39 also states that what the Lord Jesus did is what God has done.

Take a look now at what John writes in his epistles.

The apostle John also makes it clear in 1 John 2 verses 22-24 and Chapter 4 verses 2, 3, 9-15, that believing (not necessarily understanding) that God is a triune God is absolutely essential to salvation.

1 John 2.23: 'No one who denies the Son has the Father. Whoever confesses the Son has the Father also.' [ESV]

1 John 4.14-15: 'And we have seen and testify that the Father has sent the Son as Saviour of the world. Whoever confesses that Jesus is the Son of God, God abides in him, and he in God.'

We can see readily that the apostle John is a great resource to go to, when considering the character and nature of God. There are many other Scriptures that also teach this truth, but since John in his Gospel is presenting the Lord Jesus as the Son of God (see John 20.31), he goes to great lengths to distinguish between the three persons of the Godhead.

Often, he states what the Lord Jesus, the Son, said about the Father. In addition, he spends a significant amount of time telling us what the Lord Jesus said about the Holy Spirit.

An honest reading of John's Gospel only serves to convince me that God is a tripartite being. Here is a sample of references in

John's Gospel to the Father, the Son and the Spirit of God: Chapter 3.1-8, 16, 17, 31-36; 4.19-26; 5.17-47; 6.29, 32, 33, 63; 7.16, 17, 39; and through chapters 13 to17.

John also mentions the Father, the Son, and the Holy Spirit repeatedly in the Epistles that he wrote.

For example, he says in 1 John 4 verse 2, 'By this you know the Spirit of God: Every spirit (this is describing an individual's heartfelt confession) that confesses that Jesus Christ has come in the flesh is of God'. John also mentions the three Persons of the Trinity in verses 13 to 15 of the same chapter. If the Father sent His Son, verse 14, you would take for granted that the Father is one person, and the Son is one other person. Now, you might say that doesn't mean that they are both God so in our next chapter we will have to look at some Scriptures to see if the Father, the Son, and the Spirit all have the core characteristics of God.

But before we do that, notice this. In John chapter 10 when the Lord Jesus was teaching the Jews about what He did, what His Father did, and His relationship with His Father, they started to pick up stones and were about to stone Him to death (verse 31). When the Lord Jesus asks them why they are going to stone Him, the Jews answered, 'For a good work we do not stone You, but for blasphemy, and because You, being a Man, make Yourself God' (verse 33). It is very clear that the Jews knew that the Lord Jesus was claiming to be equal with His Father (and therefore God), as they intended to stone Him for blasphemy.

Finally, Paul reminds us in Ephesians chapter 2 verse 18, that 'through Him (Jesus) we both have access by one Spirit to the Father'. This reinforces the truth of the harmony of the Godhead in the work of salvation in the era in which we now live.

CHAPTER 5

The Characteristics of God

Here is our next question: In the New Testament, do the characteristics of God apply equally to the Father, the Son, and the Holy Spirit?

In this chapter we are going to highlight 12 qualities and characteristics of God and try to see if there are Scriptures which demonstrate that these features of God are indeed seen in the Father, the Son, and the Holy Spirit.

1. God is the Creator.

The Bible opens with a reference to the Holy Spirit. Genesis chapter 1 verse 2 states, 'The Spirit of God was hovering over the face of the waters'. But verse 1 says, 'In the beginning God created the heavens and the earth'. This general description of God creating runs through all of Scripture, e.g., Psalm 89.11; Psalm 90.2; Acts 17.24; Romans 1.20; Hebrews 11.3. So it is of interest to note where the other members of the Godhead, the Trinity, are clearly involved in the creation of the world.

So we have the Spirit of God mentioned as being present at creation in Genesis chapter 1 verse 2. But in Job, which incidentally is dated as one of the earliest books of the biblical canon, we read that the Spirit of God was not only present but was involved in the creation: 'The Spirit of God has made me, and the breath of the Almighty gives me life,' Job 33.4. Psalm 104 verse 30 makes a similar statement: 'You send forth Your Spirit, they are created; and You renew the face of the earth'.

As we read through the New Testament, we are faced with claims that the Son of God, the Lord Jesus Christ, was not only present at the creation but that He too was actively involved in it: John 1.1-3, Colossians 1.15-17, Hebrews 1.2.

The combined truth of these verses, and the following passages, leaves me completely convinced that Scripture is claiming full equality of the Son, the Lord Jesus Christ, with the Father (often simply described as God).

> In John chapter 1 verses 1-3, 14, 18, the Lord Jesus is described as the Creator and the revealer of God the Father.

> In Colossians chapter 1 verses 12-17, the Lord Jesus is described as the Creator and Sustainer.

> In Hebrews chapter 1 verses 1-14, the Lord Jesus is described as the Creator, the appointed heir, and the full expression of deity as revealer of and sustainer of everything. The relationship of the Son, Jesus, with the Father is emphasised. He is also the focus of angelic praise and worship. Finally, the Lord is highlighted as the one whom the Father delights to honour.

2. God is the Saviour.

The Trinity is also involved in the provision of salvation for the people of the world. When the Lord Jesus explains the need for the new birth in John chapter 3, He explains that the Father, the

Son, and the Spirit of God are all involved equally in this process (just as they were involved in the physical creation of the world).

In verse 5, He explains that to be saved and in God's kingdom (to live under His authority and to submit to and enjoy His power and protection), a person needs to be 'born of water and the Spirit'. They need the work of the Spirit of God to cleanse them and to save them. In verses 14 and 15, He shows that the death of the Son on the cross is the only basis upon which human beings can have eternal life. And, in verses 16 and 17, He highlights the love of God the Father in sending His Son into the world so that we can be saved.

As you continue to explore the New Testament Scriptures it becomes obvious that God the Father, God the Son and God the Spirit were all intimately involved in planning for and providing salvation. See Matthew 28.18-20; John 3.34-36; Romans 1.1-6; 2 Thessalonians 2.13-14; 1 Timothy 3.16; Hebrews 9.14.

In the Old Testament, God is clearly described as a Saviour God. This passage from Isaiah 45 (verses 21-22) makes this plain:

> 'Declare and present your case;
> let them take counsel together!
> Who told this long ago?
> Who declared it of old?
> Was it not I, the LORD?
> And there is no other god besides me,
> a righteous God and a Saviour;
> there is none besides me.
> Turn to me and be saved,
> all the ends of the earth!
> For I am God, and there is no other.'
>
> [ESV]

Then, in the New Testament, we find that the Lord Jesus is often described as the Saviour God. In Titus chapter 2 verses 11 to 14 we read:

> 'For the grace of God has appeared, bringing salvation for all people, training us to renounce ungodliness and worldly passions, and to live self-controlled, upright, and godly lives in the present age, waiting for our blessed hope, the appearing of the glory of our *great God and Saviour Jesus Christ*, who gave himself for us to redeem us from all lawlessness and to purify for himself a people for his own possession who are zealous for good works.' [ESV]

Paul then explains in chapter 3 verses 4 to 6 that all of the persons of the Godhead are not only involved in providing salvation, but that the Father and the Son are both described as 'our Saviour':

> 'But when the kindness and the love of *God our Saviour* toward man appeared, not by works of righteousness which we have done, but according to His mercy He saved us, through the washing of regeneration and renewing of *the Holy Spirit*, whom He poured out on us abundantly through *Jesus Christ our Saviour.*'

3. God is all-knowing (omniscient).

God is the source of all knowledge and intelligence. He knows everything in terms of facts, events and circumstances (the beginning to the end).

In Proverbs chapter 8 verse 22, King Solomon is reflecting on God's wisdom and reminds his readers that wisdom was God's before anything else existed: 'The Lord possessed me (wisdom) at the beginning of His way, before His works of old'.

The prophet Isaiah does the same thing, but in the form of a question, in chapter 40 verses 13 and 14. On this occasion he is referring to the Spirit of God when he asks, 'Who has directed the Spirit of the Lord, or as His counsellor has taught Him?'

In chapter 31 and verse 4 of his book, Job announces that God sees all his ways and assesses all his actions.

Then in chapter 34 verse 21, he makes it clear that God is constantly aware of all his activities: 'For His eyes are on the ways of man, and He sees all his steps'.

In Psalm 147 verse 5, the Psalmist describes the Lord God as 'Great ... and mighty in power; His understanding is infinite'.

Proverbs chapter 15 verse 3 explains, 'The eyes of the Lord are in every place, keeping watch on the evil and the good'.

In Matthew chapter 9 verse 4, it says of the Lord Jesus, the Son of God: '*Jesus, knowing their thoughts,* said, "Why do you think evil in your hearts?"'

Matthew continues, in chapter 12 verse 25, to explain, '*Jesus knew their thoughts*, and said to them, "Every kingdom divided against itself is brought to desolation; and every city or house divided against itself will not stand"'.

Then, in the Gospel of John chapter 2 verses 24 and 25, we read, 'But Jesus did not commit Himself to them, because *He knew all men*, and had no need that anyone should testify of man: for *He knew what was in man'*.

Then in chapter 13 verses 1 to 3: 'Now before the Feast of the

Passover, when *Jesus knew* that His hour had come that He should depart from this world to the Father, having loved His own who were in the world, He loved them to the end. And supper being ended, the devil having already put it into the heart of Judas Iscariot, Simon's son, to betray Him, *Jesus, knowing* that the Father had given all things into His hands, and that He had come from God and was going to God . . .'

The writer of Hebrews, when talking about God the Father in chapter 4 verse 13, states, 'And there is *no creature hidden from His sight*, but all things are naked and open to the eyes of Him to whom we must give account'.

The apostle John in his letters writes about God the Father In 1 John chapter 3 verse 20, he declares, 'God is greater than our heart, and *knows all things*.'

You can see how the Scriptures make clear the claim that the Father, the Son, and the Spirit, all have this characteristic of deity - omniscience (to be all-knowing).

4. God is timeless and eternal.
There was never a time when God did not exist; there will never be a time when God ceases to exist.

God is the self-existent source of all physical and spiritual life. He is the 'unbegun beginning' of all created things.

Scripture teaches that not only does the Spirit of God pre-date creation, Genesis 1.2, but that He is eternal.

Hebrews chapter 9 verse 14 asks, 'How much more shall the blood of Christ, who through *the eternal Spirit* offered Himself without spot to God, cleanse your conscience from dead works to serve the living God?'

In Isaiah 9 verse 6, the child that is born and the son that is given, i.e., the Son of God, is addressed as *'the everlasting Father'.*

Psalm 90 verse 2 states: 'Before the mountains were brought forth, or ever You had formed the earth and the world, even *from everlasting to everlasting, You are God'.*

Isaiah 40 verse 28 says: 'Have you not known? Have you not heard, *the everlasting God*, the LORD, the Creator of the ends of the earth, neither faints nor is weary. His understanding is unsearchable'.

As you can see from these verses, all three persons of the Godhead are described as *eternal.*

5. God is all-powerful, there is no limit to His power (omnipotent).

God is all-powerful, having more than enough strength to do the sum total of everything He chooses to do. We have to qualify this by saying that God will never do things that other aspects of His character exclude Him from doing, e.g., lying, Titus 1.2.

Psalms 66 verse 3 states: 'Say to God, "How awesome are Your works! Through the greatness of Your power Your enemies shall submit themselves to You"'.

In Micah chapter 3 verse 8 we read, 'But truly I am *full of power by the Spirit of the LORD,* and of justice and might, to declare to Jacob his transgression and to Israel his sin'.

The prophet Zechariah writes, 'So he answered and said to me,

"This is the word of the LORD to Zerubbabel, *Not by might, nor by power, but by My Spirit,* says the LORD of hosts'" (chapter 4 verse 6).

In Luke chapter 4 verse 14, the Lord Jesus is described as returning 'in *the power of the Spirit* to Galilee'.

Romans chapter 1 verse 4 announces the Lord Jesus as 'declared to be the Son of God with power *according to the Spirit of holiness*, by the resurrection from the dead'.

Again, in chapter 15 verse 19, we read about the power through which the apostle operated, described as 'in mighty signs and wonders, by the *power of the Spirit of God*, so that from Jerusalem and round about to Illyricum I have fully preached the gospel of Christ'.

In Revelation chapter 19 verse 6, the authority of God to reign is stated: 'For the *Lord God Omnipotent* reigns'.

Again, in 2 Corinthians chapter 6 verse 18, the term 'omnipotent' (or 'almighty') is used to show the power of God in His relationship as Father: 'I will be a Father to you, and you shall be My sons and daughters, says the LORD Almighty'.

In Revelation chapter 1 verse 8, the word is used to describe the Lord Jesus and the Father: 'I am the Alpha and the Omega, the Beginning and the End, says the Lord, who is and who was and who is to come, the Almighty'.

This characteristic of God can be seen in many other passages of Scripture: Job 42.2; Psalm 115.3; Matthew 19.26; Mark 14.36; Luke 1.37; Hebrews 13.6.

6. God is Immutable (unchangeable in character).

God never changes His nature or attributes. You can depend on Him, trust Him, and know that what He says, He will ultimately do.

When Job is talking about God, he exclaims, 'But He is unchangeable, and who can turn Him back? What He desires, that He does. For He will complete what He appoints for me, and many such things are in His mind' (Job 23.13, 14) [ESV].

In chapter 33, which we have already referred to, Job describes the actions of 'the Almighty' and the 'Spirit of God', and explains that they cannot be contested or divided, and that God acts as one in bringing about His purposes in the lives of humanity.

Numbers 23 verse 19 declares: 'God is not a man, that He should lie, nor a son of man, that He should repent. Has He said, and will He not do? Or has He spoken, and will He not make it good?'

Psalms 33 verse 11 says: 'The counsel of the LORD stands forever, the plans of His heart to all generations'.

Hebrews 1 verse 12 contrasts Creation with God: 'Like a cloak You will fold them up, and they will be changed. But You are the same, and Your years will not fail'.

Hebrews 13 verse 8 states: 'Jesus Christ is the same yesterday, today, and forever'.

7. God is unlimited geographically (omnipresent).

Each of the verses referenced below either states or implies the fact that God is not restricted by, or limited to, any physical location:

Genesis 28 verse 15: 'Behold, I am with you and will keep you wherever you go, and will bring you back to this land; for I will not leave you until I have done what I have spoken to you'.

Genesis 31 verse 3: 'Then the LORD said to Jacob,"Return to the land of your fathers and to your kindred, and I will be with you'" [ESV].

Deuteronomy 4 verse 39: 'God in heaven above and on the earth beneath'.

Joshua 1 verse 9: 'The LORD your God is with you wherever you go'.

Psalm 139 verse 7: 'Where can I go from Your Spirit?'

Isaiah 66 verse 1: 'Thus says the LORD: "Heaven is My throne, and earth is My footstool. Where is the house that you will build Me? And where is the place of My rest?"'

Jeremiah 23 verse 24: 'Do I not fill heaven and earth?'

Acts 17 verse 27: 'He is not far from each one of us'.

Hebrews 13 verse 5: 'I will never leave you nor forsake you'.

8. God is Sovereign.

God is unrestricted and unguided (apart from being guided by His moral perfection) in how He chooses to act. He acts without reference to anyone or anything.

Moses taught the children of Israel these words: 'Therefore know this day, and consider it in your heart, that the LORD Himself is God in heaven above and on the earth beneath; there is no other' (Deuteronomy 4.39).

The Psalmist says in Psalm 135 verse 5-6, 'For I know that the LORD is great, and our Lord is above all gods. Whatever the LORD pleases He does, in heaven and in earth, in the seas and in all deep places'.

Nebuchadnezzar had learned that God is absolutely sovereign, as recorded in the book of Daniel chapter 4 verse 35: 'All the inhabitants of the earth are reputed as nothing; He does according to His will in the army of heaven and among the inhabitants of the earth. No one can restrain His hand or say to Him, "What have You done?"'

As David prayed before anointing Solomon, King of Israel: 'Both riches and honour come from You, and You reign over all. In Your hand is power and might; in Your hand it is to make great and to give strength to all' (1 Chronicles 29.12).

In Psalm 47 verse 2, the sons of Korah sing, 'For the LORD Most High is awesome; He is a great King over all the earth'.

The statements of Psalm 83 verse 18 and Psalm 93 verse 1 confirm these statements to be true.

9. God is Truth.

God is absolute truth. To know Him is to know reality.

Moses describes God in Deuteronomy chapter 32 verse 4 as 'The Rock, His work is perfect; for all His ways are justice, a God of truth and without injustice; righteous and upright is He'.

David says of God, in 2 Samuel chapter 7 verse 28, 'And now, O Lord GOD, You are God, and Your words are true, and You have promised this goodness to Your servant'.

Psalm 33 verses 4-5 states, 'For the word of the LORD is right, and all His work is done in truth. He loves righteousness and justice; the earth is full of the goodness of the LORD'.

It is said of the Lord Jesus, in John chapter 1 verse 14, that He is 'full of grace and truth', while in John chapter 14 verse 6, He states that He is 'the way, the truth, and the life '.

The Lord Jesus also describes the Holy Spirit, in John chapter 14 verse 17, as 'the Spirit of truth'. Finally, in John chapter 17 verse 17 when addressing the Father in prayer, He requests, 'Sanctify them by Your truth. Your word is truth'.

10. God is Righteous.

He always does and is what is right. He is the standard of all that is perfect. He is morally right in every way without any hint of deviousness. Read the exclamations about God's righteousness by various Bible authors:

> Ezra 9 verse 15: 'You are righteous ... no one can stand before You because of this!'

> Psalm 48 verse 10: 'Your right hand is full of righteousness'.

> Psalm 119 verse 137: 'Righteous are You, O LORD, and upright are Your judgments'.

> Psalm 145 verse 17: 'The LORD is righteous in all His ways, gracious in all His works'.

> Jeremiah 23 verse 5: 'I will raise to David a Branch of righteousness'; verse 6: 'The LORD our righteousness'.

1 John 2 verse 29: 'He is righteous ... Everyone who practises righteousness is born of Him'.

The New Testament makes statements that confirm that the Lord Jesus is also described as righteous, just as God the Father is, e.g.,

'Even the righteousness of God, through faith in Jesus Christ, to all and on all who believe. For there is no difference' (Romans 3.22).

'For Christ is the end of the law for righteousness to everyone who believes' (Romans 10.4).

'My little children, these things I write to you, so that you may not sin. And if anyone sins, we have an Advocate with the Father, Jesus Christ the righteous' (1 John 2.1).

The Spirit of God is also described as being righteous and is the source of righteousness for the believer:

'That the righteous requirement of the law might be fulfilled in us who do not walk according to the flesh but according to the Spirit ... And if Christ is in you, the body is dead because of sin, but the Spirit is life because of righteousness' (Romans 8.4, 10).

'For the fruit of the Spirit is in all goodness, righteousness, and truth' (Ephesians 5.9).

11. God is Just.

What God does is always fair. He executes perfect justice in keeping with His righteousness.

In Deuteronomy 32 verse 4, Moses states about God, 'He is the

Rock, His work is perfect; for all His ways are justice, a God of truth and without injustice; righteous and upright is He'.

Isaiah writes about God in chapter 45 verse 21, describing Him as a just God and a Saviour.

This attribute is also applied to the Lord Jesus in 1 Peter chapter 3 verse 18: 'For Christ also suffered once for sins, the just for the unjust, that He might bring us to God, being put to death in the flesh but made alive by the Spirit'.

All the members of the Godhead, Father, Son, and Holy Spirit, are referred to in Isaiah chapter 11 verses 1-10 as being just in ruling the world in a coming day.

12. God is Love.

God is perfect, infinite love. He loves in spite of the character of the recipient. Love needs someone to love, so the very fact that God is eternal and existed before anything else existed means that there had to be someone to love before humans were created. So, whom did God love? We would all agree that love is a basic feature of the character of God so He had to have someone to love. The Father loved the Son, the Spirit of God loved the Father, the Son loved the Spirit, the Son loved the Father, the Father loved the Spirit, and the Spirit loved the Son.

Listen to the teaching of the Lord Jesus about His Father in Matthew chapter 5 verses 43-48:

> 'You have heard that it was said, "You shall love your neighbour and hate your enemy". But I say to you, Love your enemies ... and pray for those who ... persecute you, that you may be sons of your Father in heaven; for He makes His sun

rise on the evil and on the good, and sends rain on the just and on the unjust. For if you love those who love you, what reward have you? Do not even the tax collectors do the same? And if you greet your brethren only, what do you do more than others? Do not even the tax collectors do so? Therefore you shall be perfect, just as your Father in heaven is perfect.'

It would be worthwhile reading through John 13 to 17 at this stage. These passages are full of references to the love of the Father and the love of the Son. Let me draw your attention to a few of them:

In John chapter 13 verse 1, we are explicitly told about the love of the Lord Jesus for His disciples: 'Now before the Feast of the Passover, when Jesus knew that His hour had come that He should depart from this world to the Father, having loved His own who were in the world, He loved them to the end'.

John records the words of the Lord Jesus about the Father's love in chapter 14 verses 21-26:

'He who has My commandments and keeps them, it is he who loves Me. And he who loves Me will be loved by My Father, and I will love him and manifest Myself to him. Judas (not Iscariot) said to Him, "Lord, how is it that You will manifest Yourself to us, and not to the world?" Jesus answered and said to him, "If anyone loves Me, he will keep My word; and My Father will love him, and We will come to him and make our home with him. He who does not love Me does not keep My words; and the word which you hear is not Mine but the Father's who sent me. These things I have spoken to you while being present with you. But the Helper, the Holy Spirit, whom the Father will send in My name, He will teach you all things, and bring to your remembrance all things that I said to you."'

There are many other references to the love of the Father and the love of the Son in John's Gospel. This theme continues through the New Testament letters and it would be worthwhile looking for these passages. Here are a few to get you started:

Galatians 2 verse 20: 'I have been crucified with Christ; it is no longer I who live, but Christ lives in me; and the life which I now live in the flesh I live by faith in the Son of God, who loved me and gave Himself for me'.

Romans 5 verse 8: 'God demonstrates His own love toward us, in that while we were still sinners, Christ died for us'.

Ephesians 2 verse 4: 'But God, who is rich in mercy, because of His great love with which He loved us ...'

1 John 3 verse 1: 'Behold what manner of love ...'

1 John 4 verses 9-16: 'In this the love of God was manifested toward us ... in this is love ... God is love'.

Finally, in this section, we can be assured that the Spirit of God also demonstrated this great feature of deity. Here are two references to support this:

Romans 15 verse 30: 'I beg you, brethren, through the Lord Jesus Christ, and through the love of the Spirit, that you strive together with me in prayers to God for me'.

Galatians 5 verse 22: 'But the fruit of the Spirit is love, joy, peace, longsuffering, kindness, goodness, faithfulness'.

CHAPTER 6

The Lord Jesus
"Digging Deeper"

We have established that the Bible teaches that God is one Being, made up of three persons. It is commonly accepted that the most obvious person of the Godhead is God, or, as we have discovered the New Testament Scriptures usually call Him, 'the Father'.

Now we have some more work to do to see what the Scriptures say about (1) the Lord Jesus, and (2) The Holy Spirit.

We will be focusing on what is written about each of them in respect to the claim that they are equally God. We have two longer chapters now, the first one about the Lord Jesus Christ.

The Person of Christ

I would like to look at what the Bible teaches about this person who is the Son of God. We will consider three things in three separate sections of this longer chapter:

1. His person and character before He came to earth;
2. His person and character while living upon earth;
3. His person and character now that He is back in heaven.

It is not that the Lord Jesus is a different person at each stage. He is always the Son of God, but we need to see what the Scriptures say about Him. We also need to remember that divine persons (the Father, the Son, and the Holy Spirit) are complex, which means we don't understand everything about Them. What we do know is what They have chosen to reveal to us through the Holy Scriptures.

It is important that we know what we believe about the Saviour, why we believe it, and that it can established from Scripture, i.e., it is not just our tradition.

SECTION 1. His person and character before He came to earth

Let's think first of all about what the Lord Jesus had to say about Himself.

In John chapter 6, the people were debating as to whether Jesus was the Messiah. The whole of the chapter makes very interesting reading. It clearly records that the Lord Jesus claimed that He came from heaven and didn't start His existence when He was born on earth. All genuine Christians believe these claims. - see verses 33, 38, 40 etc.

In verse 27, He claimed the title 'Son of man', which He knew was a title reserved for Messiah. We read of this in Daniel chapter 7 verse 13, when the Son of Man comes to the Ancient of Days. The Rabbis and Jewish teachers believed that these verses spoke of the coming Messiah. In Matthew chapter 24 verse 30, Jesus predicted His own return to earth in the future and saw Himself fulfilling the ancient predictions of Daniel, Zechariah, and many of the other prophets.

Jesus also claimed that He had come from God and would return to God, as recorded in John chapter 13 verse 3: 'Jesus knowing ... that He had come from God and was going to God'.

John records the claims of Jesus, in chapter 8 verse 56, that Abraham had rejoiced at His coming into the world. The Lord Jesus is claiming that He existed prior to His birth in Bethlehem. In the first statement He says, 'Abraham rejoiced to see My day'. The Jews questioned how this could be as He wasn't even 50 years old at the time. They point out He was living a long time after Abraham.

When you read about the life of Abraham in the book of Genesis, you will come across a very interesting story in chapter 18. First of all, we read in verse 1 that the LORD appeared to Abraham. Reading right through the chapter makes it very clear that this was a physical appearance of God (the LORD) to Abraham. There are three men who come to Abraham, two are angels and one is the LORD Himself. As we follow the story line, we find that we are listening in to a conversation. It is almost as if the LORD is talking to Himself. But in light of the other passages we have referred to, when God is talking, it is most likely that the members of the Godhead are talking to each other.

God promises to return to Sarah at the appropriate time and that she will have a son (v.14). This reminds us that God holds life in His hand. In this situation it is even more amazing since Sarah is past the age when she would expect to be having children.

Then the LORD makes a statement, 'Shall I hide from Abraham what I am doing?' (v.17). This is when God warns Abraham that He is going to judge the cities of Sodom and Gomorrah. Abraham stands before the Lord (v.22) and asks the momentous question, 'Would You also destroy the righteous with the wicked?' (v.23), and ends the conversation by making a statement about God's character, 'Shall not the Judge of all the earth do right?' (v.25).

I wonder if this is when Abraham got an insight into the coming of Messiah, whom we now know as the Lord Jesus Christ. We know from two other Scriptures that the Lord Jesus will be the appointed Judge of the world.

> Acts 17 verse 31: 'He will judge the world in righteousness by the Man whom He has ordained'.

> John 5 verse 22: 'The Father judges no one, but has committed all judgment to the Son'.

It could also be that Abraham understood that God would bring a promised Messiah in to the world, when he learned that through him the world would be blessed (Genesis 12.1-3).

John records in chapter 8 verse 58 that Jesus said, 'Before Abraham was, I AM'. This is an amazing statement by the Lord Jesus. He is using the name which God told Moses about in Exodus chapter 3 verse 14. He is claiming that He is the great 'I am' of the Old Testament. The people of His day knew exactly what He meant as their immediate reaction was to stone Him. This was the normal method of capital punishment for blasphemy. If, however, they had looked at the evidence (the fulfilment of the prophecies and predictions of the Old Testament), they would have seen that His claims stood up to scrutiny and were genuine.

These are all bold statements, leaving us with no doubt that the Lord Jesus believed that He was from another world, and equal with God, the Father and the Spirit.

Now there are some very interesting incidents in the Old Testament that we need to look at. The only logical explanation for each of them is that God the Son appeared to men at various times well in advance of Him taking a body permanently after He was conceived in the womb of Mary. These are often called pre-incarnate appearances of the Son of God, i.e., before He was born at Bethlehem and called Jesus. This is similar to what we have looked at when the LORD appeared to Abraham in Genesis 18. As we look at them, I am going to ask you some questions which hopefully will cause you to think.

So here are some of the Old Testament Scriptures which describe appearances of God in a physical form.

Genesis 32.24-32: My Question - *Whom did Jacob wrestle with?*

Genesis 32.1 states that 'the angels of God' met Jacob, but in verse 30 Jacobs exclaims, 'I have seen God face to face'. So, he clearly felt that this was more than just an appearance of an angel or angels. John chapter 1 verse 18 says, 'No one has seen God at any time. The only begotten Son, who is in the bosom of the Father, He has declared Him'. Am I right in understanding from this verse that any physical appearance of God is always through an appearance of the Son of God? I am sure that this is the case.

Hosea chapter 12 verse 4 makes it clear who is being described in Genesis 32. In verse 3, Hosea writes that Jacob had power with God, and in verse 4 he says that Jacob had power over the Angel. But in verse 5, the Angel is described as the LORD GOD of Hosts, leading us to believe that this was an appearance of God in a physical form.

Joshua 5.13-15: My Question - *Who is the Captain of the Host?*

Joshua was the second leader that Israel had as a nation after they left Egypt. He was the military commander as well as the political leader of the nation. He had been brought up and trained by Moses, who was possibly the greatest leader that Israel had ever known. Joshua had witnessed national slavery and the oppression of his people, but he lived to see the deliverance that Jehovah had given them. Chapter 5 of his book records further momentous events as Joshua brings the nation across the dry river bed of the Jordan, circumcises the Israelite men, and oversees the nation celebrating the first Passover in 'the promised land'.

These were unique occasions - the manna that had been provided every day in the Wilderness all of a sudden stopped. They enjoyed eating roasted grain from a harvest that they had not worked for. Everything seemed to be going so well, when all of a sudden Joshua is confronted by a warrior with sword drawn and ready for battle. Joshua challenges this warrior: 'Are you friend or foe?'; 'Are you for us or for our enemies?' To his great surprise the warrior replied, 'No, but as Commander of the army of the LORD I have now come' (v 14).

Who is this? Is it an appearance of God in physical form? I think so!

Joshua 13.2-21: My Question - *Who appeared to Manoah and his wife?*

Note the expression 'the Angel of the LORD' in verse 3 of this passage. This is not just an angel of the Lord but the person who appears is specifically called '***the*** Angel of the LORD'.

Put this phrase, 'the angel of the Lord', into any Bible app or a concordance, and read the various stories where it is used. I have come to the conclusion that it is usually describing an appearance of God in physical form. Remember that the word 'angel' can simply be translated as 'messenger', and maybe that will help us understand who is appearing to these different people.

The prediction of the birth of a child that is given to Manoah's wife could only come from a supernatural source due to the type of information that is provided (eventually Manoah meets this Person as well, 13.13).

Later on in the story, the woman describes the Angel of the Lord as 'very awesome' and when both husband and wife have a final meeting with the Angel, they ask for a name. The answer they get is that it is 'wonderful'. Now this is very interesting. The word 'wonderful' can be translated 'incomprehensible, extraordinary, remarkable, beyond understanding'. It is the same word that is used to express how difficult it is for humans to know God in Psalm 139 verse 6: 'Such knowledge is too wonderful for me: it is high, I cannot attain it'. It is a similar word to the one used in Isaiah chapter 9 verse 6 to describe the coming Messiah (the Lord Jesus) as 'Wonderful, Counsellor, Mighty God'.

Was this another temporary appearance of the Son of God? I think so!

Proverbs 8.30: My Question - *Is this speaking of the Lord Jesus?*

The book of Proverbs is one of the 'wisdom' books in the Bible and while all of the chapters bring us wise advice and guidance, chapter 8 is an appeal by Solomon to listen to the voice of wisdom. The more I have read this chapter the more convinced I become that it is speaking about the Lord Jesus Christ, the Son of God. William MacDonald in the *Believer's Bible Commentary* says this: 'These passages dealing with Wisdom can be fittingly applied to the Lord Jesus, since the New Testament refers to Him as Wisdom (Matthew 11.19; Luke 11.49; 1 Corinthians 1.24, 30; Colossians 2.3)'. Verses 30 and 31 are the climax of the chapter where wisdom is described as a person who was resident with God (the Father) in heaven. As with most passages like this, there are a couple of phrases that are difficult to explain, but I think that it is fair to say that these words can be applied to the Lord Jesus.

The general statements in the early part of the chapter can equally be applied to the Lord Jesus, but I am thinking in particular about the later verses. For instance:

Verses 15-16: 'By me kings reign, and rulers decree justice'. Daniel recalls that King Nebuchadnezzar had to learn this. He records in Daniel chapter 4 verse 17, 'In order that the living may know that the Most High rules in the kingdom of men, gives it to whomever He will, and sets over it the lowest of men'.

In verses 22-31, wisdom is described as pre-dating the creation of the universe and He (wisdom) is described as being beside the Creator as a master craftsman who delighted the Creator on a daily basis (v.30). This agrees, of course, with references in John chapter 1 verse 3, Colossians chapter 1 verse 16, and Hebrews chapter 1 verse 2, where the Lord Jesus is also described as the Creator.

The beautiful relationship between these two persons is evident in these verses as the writer describes the joy and delight that they have in each other's company, and the ecstatic feelings that Wisdom has when He reflects on the place (earth) and the people (the sons of earth/Adam) that God (the Father) has created.

Once again, I come to the conclusion that this passage can only be referring to the Lord Jesus.

Daniel 3.25: My Question - *Who was in the fire with Shadrach, Meshach and Abednego?*

This is a great story. I don't mean that it is just an interesting tale, but that it is the record of a very interesting event that took place in the life of the great Babylonian King, Nebuchadnezzar. You will need to read the whole of Daniel chapter three to get the background. Let me pick up the story where the three men, Shadrach, Meshach and Abednego (as they had been renamed by the Babylonians, see Daniel 1.7) have been thrown into a blazing furnace of fire. This was punishment by the Babylonian king for their refusal to bow down to his idolatrous image. Suddenly the king is on his feet and calling for his advisors: 'Did we throw three men into the furnace, or four?' He is assured that they threw in only three men. 'But there are four in the furnace now,' he exclaims, 'and one of them is like a god.' What Nebuchadnezzar thought a god would look like, we don't know, but whatever he saw, it appeared to him as a divine or supernatural being.

The only explanation that I can think of for this event is that the Son of God came down in person to support and protect these servants of God in their time of suffering. He does the same today today, as He has promised in Hebrews chapter 13 verses 5-8, "'I will never leave you nor forsake you." So we may boldly say: "The Lord is my helper; I will not fear. What can man do to me?" Remember those who rule over you, who have spoken the word of God to you, whose faith follow, considering the outcome of their conduct. Jesus Christ is the same yesterday, today, and forever'.

Again, in Daniel 3, this is another temporary appearance of the Son of God, as in each of these Old Testament passages we have considered.

Next, in section 2, we are going to consider the character of the Lord Jesus while He lived on earth.

SECTION 2: His person and character while living upon earth

In this section, we are going think about Jesus, the Son of God - His incarnation, His humanity, and the demonstration of His deity. To do this, we will be considering three related questions:

> What did He do while on earth?
> What was He like?
> Why did He come?

The humanity of the Lord Jesus was obvious when He lived on earth, so people required proof of His deity.

His deity may seem more obvious now (with the evidence of Scripture, history and hindsight), but we need historical evidence and proof of His actual life on earth, His humanity.

So, what did He do while on earth, and why, and what was He like?

1. *He manifested God in flesh* - He was God among men as a man.

The claim of Scripture is that Jesus was God come to earth in a body, *'God was manifest in flesh'*. The first Gospel, Matthew, in chapter 1, gives the account of 'the angel of the Lord' appearing to Joseph to prevent him from breaking his betrothal to Mary. The angel explains, 'That which is conceived in her is of the Holy Spirit'. The natural method of conception is a man and woman coming together, with the man determining the gender of the child. Now Joseph is being told that this child is different. He is 'of the Holy Spirit'. God was miraculously bringing His Son into the womb of Mary. The following verses in this chapter, quoting from the Old Testament Scriptures, clearly indicate this was a long-term plan which was being fulfilled in the birth of Jesus. It is interesting that the name Emmanuel (v.23) is in the Old Testament prophecy quoted from Isaiah chapter 7 verse 14. It means 'God with us'. It is very significant that Messiah is described as being God present on earth.

Other Scriptures which support this point are 1 Timothy 3.16, Colossians 2.9.

2. *He displayed the glory and honour that is seen in perfect humanity.*

In Hebrews chapter 2 verse 9, the Lord Jesus is described as being 'made a little lower than the angels, for the suffering of death'. As God, He could not die, so He steps down and takes His place as a man so that He can suffer and die for sin, and in so doing provide salvation. The verse also describes the Lord Jesus as 'crowned with glory and honour'. Some may see this as a reflection of

His deity, but it seems to be more consistent with the previous verses to understand that it is describing the Lord Jesus taking His place as a man. Notice that verse 7 describes Adam, the first man, in the same way - lower than angels, crowned with glory and honour, and put in charge of the creation.

The Lord Jesus becomes a perfect man displaying and demonstrating how man should have acted and bringing His Father great pleasure in so doing. It is no wonder that God broke His silence after Jesus was baptised in the river Jordan to announce, 'This is My beloved Son, in whom I am well pleased' (Matthew 3.17).

3. He fully experienced human suffering and learned obedience

When we read the Scriptures, we need to be careful not to read into a verse something that is not there. For instance, Hebrews chapter 2 verse 10 states that the Lord Jesus experienced suffering in life to make Him perfect. Different translations will express this slightly differently but essentially they say the same thing. You might read this and think - so Jesus was not perfect and He had to go through certain sufferings and experiences to refine Him so he would be perfect at the end of the day. But there are so many other Scriptures that teach clearly that He was holy, blameless, and unstained by sin, so this verse cannot mean that. The idea in this verse is that as the Son of God in heaven, He had never experienced suffering before. It was not part of His experience, and so as a result of suffering He became complete and fully rounded in His experiences of life. We will see in a later section that this has fitted Him to understand all that we experience in life.

There is another similar expression in Hebrews chapter 5 verses 7-9. In these verses, we are given a glimpse of the agony which the Lord Jesus experienced when facing crucifixion. We see tears pouring down His face as He pleads with His Father about the awful death He is about to know. The explanation given is, 'Though He was a Son, yet He learned obedience by the things which He suffered'. This verse reminds us that the man suffering in the garden of Gethsemane was the Son of God. It also concludes that His suffering and agony brought Him in His experience to a place where He had never been before. It is not saying that He was ever disobedient, but that He had never been in circumstances where He had to be obedient before. He learned what obedience felt like and was brought to another point of mature experience as a man (v.9).

4. *He experienced life so that He could empathise and sympathise.*

Later in this chapter we will be thinking about what the Lord Jesus is doing for His people now that He is back in heaven. One of the important reasons for Him coming to earth was to live a normal life so that He could understand how we feel. His primary reason for coming was to provide salvation through His death, burial, and resurrection. But those who trust Him can now experience His strength, His sympathy and His care in all the circumstances that they go through in life. Hebrews chapter 4 verse 15 reminds us that the Lord Jesus faced all the same trying circumstances that we face. He had no tendency, indeed no ability, to sin, being the perfect Son of God, but He still faced the problems that we all come across in life. Hebrews 5 verses 2, 8 and 9 make the same point.

5. *He was intentionally fulfilling prophecy.*

You do not need to read Matthew's Gospel for too long before you notice the phrase, 'that it might be fulfilled', coming up time and time again, e.g., Matthew 1.22; 27.35. In the Gospels, the historical accounts of the earthly life of the Lord Jesus unite prophecy with reality. What was written hundreds, and sometimes thousands, of years before, was literally being fulfilled before people's eyes. This is not something that can be manipulated or manufactured. Only someone who had greater powers than a normal man could arrange the place of His birth, the time of His death, the method of His execution, so that it fits with something that was written long before He lived on earth. The fact that these predictions were written in the Hebrew Scriptures, and accepted by the Jews, only adds to the credibility of these claims. Some claim that the Christian part of the Bible was written and rewritten to support these claims but there is no evidence whatsoever to support this theory. We may find it hard to understand how this all works out, but it all points to the fact that the Bible is the inspired Word of God, and that Jesus of Nazareth was actually the Son of God.

6. *He displayed the love and kindness of God.*

There is an interesting little book in the New Testament called 'The Epistle of Paul to Titus'. In this letter, Paul makes a big case for God being a Saviour. He highlights this fact in every chapter - 1.3, 2.10, 2.13, 3.4, 3.6. I think it is significant that both God the Father and Jesus Christ are described in the same way, 'our Saviour'. There are two more things to notice from this book. In chapter 2, Paul talks about the Lord Jesus as, 'the great God and our Saviour Jesus Christ' [AV]. He writes in such a way that it is impossible to ignore the fact that he is telling us that the Lord Jesus is both 'our great God' and 'our Saviour'. In the final chapter he says this, 'The kindness and love of God our Saviour toward man appeared' (3.4). What is he saying? He is making it clear, as he does in chapter 2, that the Lord Jesus is God. The question is: When did the love and kindness of God our Saviour toward man appear? It was revealed when the Son of God, Jesus, was born. In His life He revealed what God was really like, for He is God.

7. He demonstrated the power of God in His miracles.

The Lord Jesus did many miracles during His three years of public ministry. The apostle John concludes his gospel by saying, 'This is the disciple who testifies of these things, and wrote these things; and we know that his testimony is true. And there are also many other things that Jesus did, which if they were written one by one, I suppose that even the world itself could not contain the books that would be written. Amen' (John 21.24-25). John is telling us that we have only a sample of the miracles that the Lord Jesus performed. He makes the same claim in chapter 20 verses 30 and 31: 'And truly Jesus did many other signs in the presence of His disciples, which are not written in this book; but these are written that you may believe that Jesus is the Christ, the Son of God; and that believing you may have life in His name'. One of the reasons for doing miracles (apart from the obvious one to help people), was to demonstrate that Jesus was more than just a man, rather God become man, supporting His claims to deity. Other verses, such as Acts 2 verse 22 and 10 verse 38, confirm that God the Father was pleased with what He did and God was with Him.

8. He proved that He was without sin and perfect, therefore the right one to be the Saviour.

The Bible predicted, in Isaiah chapter 42, that when Messiah came He would behave in such a way that it would delight the heart of God (v.1), that He would have God's Spirit (v.1), and never fail or be discouraged (v.4). Anyone who reads the record of Jesus' life (whether biblical or secular) will discover that there are no negative comments about Him. I mean none! He is recorded as being sinless and perfect in every area of life. No other human has ever achieved this, as we all do wrong and were born with a defective nature. The Lord Jesus even went as far as to challenge those who criticised Him by asking them, 'Which of you convicts Me of sin?' (John 8.46). The legal statement of the judge (Pilate) at His trial was, 'I have found no fault in this Man' (Luke 23.14), and the confession of one of the criminals who was crucified on the same day as Jesus was, 'This Man has done nothing wrong' (v.41).

A number of years after Jesus had died, risen from the dead, and gone back to heaven, the book we call Hebrews was written for new believers from a Jewish background. In this book the Lord Jesus is once again declared to be perfect in His character and behaviour: 'For such a High Priest was fitting for us, who is holy, harmless, undefiled, separate from sinners, and has become higher than the heavens' (Hebrews 7.26).

All of this was recorded so that we would understand that Jesus was the only person who ever lived who could pay for our sins, because He was without sin. Peter writes, 'For Christ also suffered once for sins, the just for the unjust, that He might bring us to God, being put to death in the flesh but made alive by the Spirit' (1 Peter 3.18).

9. *He died a sacrificial death as an act of redemption to purchase salvation.*

As stated earlier in this book, the Son of God had to become a man so that He could die for sin. In Colossians chapter 1 we read the following statements about the Lord Jesus: 'For it pleased the Father that in Him all the fullness should dwell, and by Him to reconcile all things to Himself, by Him, whether things on earth or things in heaven, having made peace through the blood of His cross. And you, who once were alienated and enemies in your mind by wicked works, yet now He has reconciled in the body of His flesh through death, to present you holy, and blameless, and above reproach in His sight' (vv.19-22). Notice the expression, 'in the body of His flesh through death'. The Lord Jesus became a man so that He could die, and, as a result, those who trust Him are reconciled to God.

There are many other verses that teach this principle, such as 1 Peter 2 verse 24 and Hebrews 2 verses 9, 14.

Please note that His death also produced many other results such as the following, although they are not the focus of this book:

He passed judgment on Satan (which will be implemented at a future date), Hebrews 2.14.

He delivered those who trust Him from the fear of death, Hebrews 2.15.

He will reconcile all things to Himself, Colossians 1.20.

He made peace, Colossians 1.20.

He declares that God is just and justifies those who believe, Romans 3.26.

He is bringing many sons to glory, Hebrews 2.10.

Here are some sample verses that clearly show the genuineness of the humanity of the Lord Jesus:

John 4.6: 'Being wearied from His journey'.

Matthew 8.24: 'But He was asleep'.

John 19.28: 'I thirst', also John 4.7 'Give Me a drink'.

Matthew 4.2: 'He was hungry'.

Now here are some verses where the Lord Jesus is spoken of as God and man:

The apostle John says he and others heard Him, saw Him, watched Him and touched Him, but a couple of lines later he says about Jesus that He is 'that eternal life which was with the Father and was manifested to us' (1 John 1.1, 2).

The essential truth here is that Jesus (the man) is the Christ (the anointed Messiah who was promised by God the Father). The Father and the Son are linked here, and John says that you can't believe in the one without the other (1 John 2.22, 23).

Again, in 1 John 3 verse 23, the apostle John says that the commandment of God the Father is that you 'believe on the name of His Son Jesus Christ'. Note the constant matching of the name Jesus, the man, with Christ, the Messiah, the 'ancient of days', as in Daniel 7 verse 13. The same verse refers to the Son of Man. This is a name that Jesus often used about Himself and is used for the same Being who is called 'the ancient of days' (v.22).

In 1 John 4 verse 2, John explains that true faith is found in those who confess, 'Jesus Christ has come in the flesh'. Notice the terminology - Jesus Christ (Messiah) has come in the flesh (taking human form).

These verses are key to this topic. In verses 14 and 15 we learn: 'The Father has sent the Son', and 'Whoever confesses that Jesus is the Son of God' has come into a relationship with God. Again you can notice the mixing of these facts that Jesus is the Son of God, and that the Father has sent the Son.

The challenge about salvation is based upon what you believe about the Lord Jesus. John concludes his letter by restating these facts, 'Whoever believes that Jesus is the Christ is born of God' (1

John 5.1). Again, in verse 5, he states, 'Who is he who overcomes the world, but he who believes that Jesus is the Son of God?'

John certainly believed that Jesus really was God become man. Jesus lost nothing of His power as God when He lived on earth. He limited His use of His divine characteristics, and experienced life for all the reasons stated above. But He was truly God and truly man, not one person divided in two, but fully God and fully man in one body. Colossians chapter 2 verse 9 sums it up very clearly, 'For in Him dwells all the fullness of the Godhead bodily'.

Hopefully, you will read this section more than once and reflect on the claims the Bible is making about the Lord Jesus. One additional passage you should read is Philippians 2 verses 5-11. Much has been written about what this passage is teaching, but as you read it for yourself, look out for statements that emphasise the genuineness of His deity (that Jesus is God), and statements that define the servant nature of His humanity. Both are essentially true about the Lord Jesus.

SECTION 3: His person and character now that He is back in heaven

From time to time you may wonder what the Lord Jesus is doing now in heaven. Before He was born, He was a 'Spirit being' who sometimes appeared on earth in physical form. We thought about that in Section 1 of this chapter. After His death, burial and resurrection (1 Corinthians 15.3-4), He ascended to heaven (Luke 24.51, Acts 1.9), and once again is based there (if I am permitted to use such an expression), but what is He doing? Is it just the same as He did before He came to earth, or has He taken on additional responsibilities? I think the answer is in the latter statement, and that is what I want to explore in Section 3 of this chapter.

Firstly, we will look at six things that we are told that He is doing. After that we will consider some general things the Lord Jesus does, and then some more specific things that He is doing for believers.

Six specific things the Lord Jesus did on returning to heaven

1. He went to heaven to prepare a place for believers.

In John chapter 14 verses 2 and 3, the Lord Jesus told His disciples that He was going to His Father's house, i.e., heaven, and that He was going to prepare a place for them. It is generally accepted that the Lord did not mean that He was going to get heaven ready in a physical sense, but that by His death, burial and resurrection He was making it possible that those who believe in Him would one day live with Him in heaven, see John chapter 17 verse 24. In effect, we see that in one sense the place (location) was prepared by His going. Hebrews chapter 9 verse 24 states that the Lord Jesus has gone 'into heaven itself, now to appear in the presence of God for us'.

2. He sat down.

The second thing we learn from Hebrews chapter 1 verse 3. The Son of God sat down upon returning to heaven: 'When He had by Himself purged our sins, sat down at the right hand of the Majesty on high'. The significance of this is that priests never sat down while serving God in the tabernacle or the temple. The Hebrew writer when commenting on the death of Christ says this, 'But this Man, after He had offered one sacrifice for sins forever, sat down at the right hand of God' (Hebrews 10.12). The work of salvation is complete, a full and final offering for sins has been made, and so the Lord Jesus is officially seated in heaven. This fits with the words of Psalm 110 verse 1, where the Father says to the Son, 'Sit at My right hand, till I make Your enemies Your footstool'. In Matthew chapter 22 verses 41 to 46, the Lord Jesus confirms that this statement was the Father talking to the Son.

3. He was glorified.

The verses that we have just referred to from Psalm 110 predict that the Son of God was going to rest (v.1), rule (v.2) and be powerful (v.3). Other Scriptures make it very clear that, upon returning to heaven, the Lord Jesus was exalted and glorified. The words of Psalm 24 from verse 7 have been given two meanings and both are possible. The picture is of a victorious king returning to his capital city. The welcome is overwhelming. The returning victor is described as the 'King of glory'. The question is asked, 'Who is this King of glory?' And the answer is given, 'The LORD strong and mighty, the LORD mighty in battle'. It is hard to see that these words refer to anyone else apart from the Lord Jesus. The debatable question is: Where is He entering? Some say that it is heaven, some say that it is Jerusalem. I am more convinced that it is heaven due to the gates to the city being described as 'everlasting doors', but I agree that it could be Jerusalem. If it is the latter, this will not take place until the Lord Jesus returns to reign on earth. But, if it is the former, this was the glorious and majestic welcome that the Lord Jesus would have received on His ascension back to heaven. Both are true, as the Saviour was exalted on His return to heaven and will be exalted when comes to earth in 'power and great glory' (Matthew 24.30).

Here are some other passages which explain that the Lord was exalted and glorified on His return to heaven:

Acts 2.33: 'Therefore being exalted to the right hand of God'.

Acts 3.13: 'The God of Abraham, Isaac, and Jacob, the God

of our fathers, glorified His Servant Jesus, whom you delivered up and denied in the presence of Pilate, when he was determined to let Him go'.

Ephesians 1.20-23: 'Which He worked in Christ when He raised Him from the dead and seated Him at His right hand in the heavenly places, far above all principality and power and might and dominion, and every name that is named, not only in this age but also in that which is to come. And He put all things under His feet, and gave Him to be head over all things to the church, which is His body, the fullness of Him who fills all in all'.

4. He became a Great High Priest.

One of the additional roles that the Lord Jesus has now is that of Great High Priest. Hebrews chapter 4 verse 14 states, 'We have a great High Priest who has passed through the heavens, Jesus the Son of God'.

Again in Hebrews 5.5 we read, 'So also Christ did not glorify Himself to become High Priest, but it was He who said to Him: "You are My Son, Today I have begotten You." As He also says in another place: "You are a priest forever according to the order of Melchizedek"'.

In chapter 6 verses 19 and 20 of the same book, the writer tells us about 'this hope' which 'we have as an anchor of the soul, both sure and steadfast, and which enters the Presence behind the veil, where the forerunner has entered for us, even Jesus, having become High Priest forever according to the order of Melchizedek'.

If you read through the rest of the letter to the Hebrews you come across regular references to the Lord Jesus becoming a High Priest/Great High Priest.

5. He gave gifts to the church.

One of the things the Lord Jesus did when He returned to heaven was to give gifts to the church. This is explained to us in Ephesians chapter 4 verse 8 where it says, 'When He ascended on high, He led captivity captive, and gave gifts to men'. These particular gifts were given to equip believers to serve the Lord.

It is interesting to notice that all three members of the Godhead, Father, Son, and Holy Spirit, were involved in the giving of gifts to the church. In Romans chapter 12 verse 3 to 8, God the Father gives the gifts, in 1 Corinthians 12 verses 7 to 11, it is the Spirit of God who gives the gifts, and, as we have just seen in Ephesians 4, the risen and ascended Christ dispenses the gifts.

6. He gave the Holy Spirit.

Finally, John tells us a number of times in his Gospel that the Holy Spirit could not come into the world to indwell believers permanently until the Lord Jesus had returned to heaven. As all the members of the Godhead were involved in the giving of gifts to the Church, so the Father, Son, and Holy Spirit were involved in the coming of the Spirit of God into the world to commence the age of the Spirit.

In John chapter 7 verse 39, we are told that the Holy Spirit could not come at that time, 'for the Holy Spirit was not yet given, because Jesus was not yet glorified'.

Again, in chapter 15 verse 26, John writes, 'But when the Comforter is come, whom I will send unto you from the Father ... He shall testify of Me'. [AV]

But, in John chapter 16 verse 7, the Lord Jesus said to His disciples, 'Nevertheless I tell you the truth; it is expedient for you that I go away: for if I go not away, the Comforter will not come unto you; but if I depart I will send Him unto you'. [AV]

Three general things that the Lord Jesus is presently doing

1. Maintaining the universe

Hebrews chapter 1 verse 3 states that one of the things that the Lord Jesus continues to do, i.e., He was doing this before He became a man, is to maintain and uphold the universe.

2. Saving souls

The call of the Saviour continues throughout every generation. While He lived on earth, He appealed to people by saying, 'Come to Me'. As we have noted earlier, the book of Titus has many references to the Lord Jesus as Saviour. For instance, in chapter 3 verses 4 to 6 we read, 'But when the kindness and the love of God our Saviour toward man appeared, not by works of righteousness which we have done, but according to His mercy He saved us, through the washing of regeneration and renewing of the Holy Spirit, whom He poured out on us abundantly through Jesus Christ our Saviour, that having been justified by His grace we should become heirs according to the hope of eternal life'.

3. Preserving all men

The Lord Jesus is not only the Saviour of all who believe, but He also preserves all people in a very general sense. Paul writes to Timothy in 1 Timothy chapter 4 verse 10, 'Because we trust in the living God, who is the Saviour of all men, especially of those who believe'. The word 'Saviour' in this context is more the idea that He preserves, maintains and delivers people in the many difficulties that they face in life. William MacDonald in his book, the *Believer's Bible Commentary*, writes, 'God is the Saviour of all men in the sense that He preserves them in the daily providences of life. But He is also the Saviour of all men in the sense ... that He has made adequate provision for the salvation of all men. He is the Saviour of those who believe in a special way because they have availed themselves of His provision. We might say that He is the potential Saviour of all men and the actual Saviour of those who believe'.

Five specific things the Lord Jesus does for believers

1. Acting as our Intercessor - going to God for us

The Lord Jesus is the one mediator between God and men, 1 Timothy 2.5-6. This becomes very apparent when a person gets saved. As they grow as a believer they also discover that the Lord Jesus continually goes into the presence of God for them. The Lord Jesus told Peter that He had prayed for him (Luke 22.32) and when He was praying to His Father about leaving the world, as recorded in John 17, He stated that He had prayed for the disciples (v.9), and that He was also praying for generations of believers who would be saved through the preaching of the apostles (v.20). It is a wonderful thing to think that the Lord Jesus prays for me!

Read Romans chapter 8 verse 34, Hebrews chapter 7 verse 25 and Hebrews chapter 9 verse 24, and enjoy this wonderful truth for yourself.

2. Being our High Priest - coming to us from God

We have mentioned already that the Lord Jesus is our Great High Priest in heaven. I am mentioning it in this section as I would like you to think about what that involves. In Hebrews chapter 4 verses 15 and 16, we learn that because of His suffering and experiences in life, we can come to Him knowing that He will empathise with us and grant us continual access into the presence of God to 'obtain mercy and find grace to help in time of need'.

In Hebrews chapter 6 verse 20, we see the Lord Jesus described as 'the forerunner'. The idea is that He has gone into heaven in advance of us. We are guaranteed to join Him there one day, but in the meantime He is the one who sustains and assists us.

There are many other references to the High Priestly work of the Lord Jesus. As you read and reflect on them, bear in mind that the Lord Jesus wouldn't be able to understand you, if He hadn't become a man (His sympathy), but He wouldn't be able to help you if He wasn't the Son of God (His power).

3. Acting as our Advocate with the Father

This term, 'our Advocate', describes a specific way in which the Lord Jesus acts on our behalf in the presence of God. When John writes his first letter, he reminds his readers that they will sin from time to time. It should not be normal for believers to sin consistently, but John says, 'If we say that we have no sin, we deceive ourselves, and the truth is not in us' (1.8). So do not deceive yourself and don't be depressed when you do sin. God has made a way for this to be sorted out.

In the next verse, John tells us what to do when we do sin: 'If we confess our sins, He is faithful and just to forgive us our sins and to cleanse us from all unrighteousness' (1.9). So, when you sin you need to act immediately, confess and admit your sin (to God in prayer), then relax. Forgiveness is promised and you will be delivered.

Then John says this, 'My little children, these things I write to you, so that you may not sin. And if anyone sins, we have an Advocate with the Father, Jesus Christ the righteous. And He Himself is the propitiation for our sins, and not for ours only but also for the whole world' (2.1-2). John continues to look at the possibility of a Christian sinning. These verses tell us what happens in heaven when you sin, whereas chapter 1 is about what you need to do here on earth when you sin, i.e., admit, confess your sins, etc.

So, the Lord Jesus, who is in heaven, acts on your behalf when you sin. *He is qualified* to do this because He is pure and holy, He is 'Jesus Christ the righteous'. *He is willing* to represent you because He is your 'Advocate'. An advocate is one who draws alongside to act on your behalf. On this occasion He draws alongside His Father because the verse says, 'We have an Advocate *with* the Father'. *He is able* to do this because He is the propitiation for our sins (that means that He is the sacrifice or the offering. In other words, He paid for these sins already by dying on the cross).

Once again, I find these truths so thrilling, and a great blessing to my soul.

4. Functioning as the Head of the Church ('the body')

One of the outstanding truths of the Epistle of Paul to the Ephesians is that Christ is described as 'head over all things to the church, which is His body' (1.22-23).

71

Most of us understand the term, 'the Head'. If we were at school, we would use it to describe the most senior person in the school. In large businesses, it is used to describe the chief executive or chairman of the organization. If we say someone is 'heading up' something, we would usually understand that this means that they are leading and directing and ultimately responsible for the way things are done.

The descriptive terms 'head' and 'body' use the analogy of the human body and a human head. One without the other is incomplete. The body cannot function without the head. The head is incomplete without the body. In human terms, the head is the means by which the body has the ability to function. Without the direction of the head, the systems that we have in our bodies could not function, yet without the body the head is incomplete. Despite the fact that we cannot understand why God has arranged it in this way, the last verse of Ephesians 1 teaches us that the same is true in the church's relationship with Christ. The Scripture states that Christ is incomplete without the Church, and yet He is the One 'who fills all in all'.

In Matthew chapter 16, the Lord Jesus is recorded as stating, 'I will build My church' (v.18). This is the church which is composed of every believer from its commencement (on the day of Pentecost, Acts 2) until its completion, at the coming of Christ (often called the Rapture, 1 Thessalonians 4.13-18). We will deal with His current relationship with a local church next.

5. Being Lord of the Church (local)

In Revelation chapter 1, the apostle John has a vision in which he sees 'One like the Son of Man' (v.13), i.e., the risen Lord Jesus Christ, standing in the middle of seven gold lampstands. The key to what this all means is given in the final verse of the chapter, verse 20, and we discover that the seven lampstands represent seven churches that existed when John was alive.

What was the point of the vision? When you read through chapters 1 to 3 of the Book of Revelation, it looks to me that the Lord is saying that He is the Lord of the churches - in control, and the One to whom all churches are responsible. He is reminding them (and us) that He knows what is going on in each church and will hold them responsible for their beliefs and behaviour. The outstanding lessons are that He greatly values His people (His churches), that each church is individual and autonomous, that churches should be a light for Christ in the world and should reflect the glory and majesty of His person.

Yes, the Lord Jesus is in heaven but He is the 'great shepherd of the sheep' (Hebrews 13.20), and He oversees and cares for His church.

Two things the Lord Jesus will be in End Times

1. The Coming Prince of Israel

Some Old Testament books describe the Lord Jesus as the coming Prince of Israel. Daniel and Ezekiel are the main ones that come to mind. It is really exciting when you realise that there is a day coming when the Lord Jesus will come to earth the second time, and Israel will at long last recognise Him as their Messiah, Daniel 9.25, Ezekiel 44.3.

2. The Judge of all the earth

Very early on in the Scriptures, we come across God described as a Judge, Genesis 15.14, 18.25. As God's revelation progresses through the Bible, we discover that the Lord Jesus is the member of the Godhead who will judge the world, John 5.22, Acts 17.31. The One who came to be the Saviour of the world will return one day to judge the world in righteousness. The wonder to me is that we, as believers, are going to be involved in His administration on earth, both in terms of judging and reigning with Christ, 1 Corinthians 6.2, 3, Revelation 5.10, 20.6, 22.5.

As we move on into the next chapter, please remember that all of the detail we have given in this chapter is important in confirming that the Lord Jesus was more than a man, and that He had to be God manifest in flesh to do the things the Bible describes about Him.

We will look at the character of the person of the Holy Spirit in our next chapter. We will be able to establish that He is a divine person and as equally God as the Father and the Son.

CHAPTER 7

The Holy Spirit
"Digging Deeper"

We will look at biblical teaching about the Holy Spirit by asking a series of questions:

1. Is the Holy Spirit God?
2. Is the Holy Spirit a person?
3. What part does the Holy Spirit play in the revelation of God in the Bible?
4. What does the Holy Spirit do for a believer today?

Q.1: Is the Holy Spirit God?

The purpose of this chapter is to look at the Holy Spirit as a member of the Godhead, so to start doing that, please note a few Scriptures that underline the fact that He is a member of the Godhead.

Genesis 1.2	He is called the Spirit of God.
Genesis 6.3	The LORD says, 'My Spirit shall not always strive with man'.
Matthew 1.18	He is the Holy Ghost (Spirit).
John 4.24	God is Spirit.
Romans 8.9	The Spirit of Christ.
2 Corinthians 3.3	The Spirit of the living God.

As you read the Scriptures you will note the strong union between God the Father, the Son, and the Holy Spirit. As a result and as we have seen, people have come to talk about God as the Triune God or the Trinity. Gathering Scriptures together we have noted that the Trinity was involved in the creation of the world, Genesis 1.1, John 1.3, Colossians 1.16, Hebrews 1.2.

Q.2: Is the Holy Spirit a person?

First, we need to think about this: How do we know the Holy Spirit is a person? You may think that this is a strange question especially if you have been a believer for a long time. But the issue is that some people will tell you that the Holy Spirit is just a force, a power or an influence. So, first of all, it would be useful to ask, How do we know that the Father and the Son are persons? and then to apply the same standards to the Spirit of God.

The answer is that the Bible describes a person as a being who can do things that are personal and relational, such as speaking, thinking, feeling, and acting. Anyone who can do these things, such as God, angels, and human beings, is a person.

So, let's measure the Holy Spirit against these standards:

1. The Holy Spirit teaches and reminds.

'But the Helper, the Holy Spirit, whom the Father will send in My name, He will teach you all things, and bring to your remembrance all things that I said to you' (John 14.26).

'These things we also speak, not in words which man's wisdom teaches but which the Holy Spirit teaches, comparing spiritual things with spiritual' (1 Corinthians 2.13).

2. The Holy Spirit speaks.

'Then the Spirit said to Philip, "Go near and overtake this chariot"' (Acts 8.29).
'As they ministered to the Lord and fasted, the Holy Spirit said, "Now separate to Me Barnabas and Saul for the work to which I have called them"' (Acts 13.2).

3. The Holy Spirit makes decisions.

'For it seemed good to the Holy Spirit, and to us, to lay upon you no greater burden than these necessary things: that you abstain from things offered to idols, from blood, from things strangled, and from sexual immorality. If you keep yourselves from these, you will do well. Farewell.' (Acts 15.28, 29).

4. The Holy Spirit can be grieved.

'And do not grieve the Holy Spirit of God, by whom you were sealed for the day of redemption' (Ephesians 4.30).

5. The Holy Spirit can be outraged.

'Of how much worse punishment, do you suppose, will he be thought worthy who has trampled the Son of God underfoot, counted the blood of the covenant by which he was sanctified a common thing, and insulted the Spirit of grace?' (Hebrews 10.29).

6. The Holy Spirit can be lied to.

'But Peter said, "Ananias, why has Satan filled your heart to lie to the Holy Spirit and keep back part of the price of the land for yourself? While it remained, was it not your own? And after it was sold, was it not in your own control? Why have you conceived this thing in your heart? You have not lied to men but to God"' (Acts 5.3, 4).

7. The Holy Spirit can forbid or prevent human speech and plans.

'Now when they had gone through Phrygia and the region of Galatia, they were forbidden by the Holy Spirit to preach the word in Asia. After they had come to Mysia, they tried to go into Bithynia, but the Spirit did not permit them' (Acts 16.6, 7).

8. The Holy Spirit thinks deeply and has deep-rooted intelligence.

'But God has revealed them to us through His Spirit. For the Spirit searches all things, yes, the deep things of God. For what man knows the things of a man except the spirit of the man which is in him? Even so no one knows the things of God except the Spirit of God' (1 Corinthians 2.10, 11). The Spirit searches everything and comprehends God's thoughts.

9. The Holy Spirit distributes spiritual gifts.

'But one and the same Spirit works all these things, distributing to each one individually as He wills' (1 Corinthians 12.11).

10. The Holy Spirit helps us, intercedes for us, and has a mind.

'Likewise the Spirit also helps in our weaknesses. For we do not know what we should pray for as we ought, but the Spirit Himself makes intercession for us with groanings which cannot be uttered. Now He who searches the hearts knows what the mind of the Spirit is, because He makes intercession for the saints according to the will of God' (Romans 8.26,27).

11. The Spirit testifies to believers.

'The Spirit Himself bears witness with our spirit that we are children of God' (Romans 8.16).

12. The Spirit bears witness to Christ.

'But when the Helper comes, whom I shall send to you from the Father, the Spirit of truth who proceeds from the Father, He will testify of Me' (John 15.26).

13. The Spirit glorifies Christ, takes what is of Christ and declares it to believers.

'He will glorify Me, for He will take of what is Mine and declare it to you' (John 16.14).

Q.3: What part does the Holy Spirit play in the revelation of God in the Bible?

The Bible starts with a reference to the Spirit of God moving on the face of the deep (Genesis 1.2), and it ends with a reference to the Holy Spirit in Revelation chapter 22 verse 17, where it states, 'And the Spirit and the bride say, "Come"'.

In between those two points, we see the revelation of God to humanity. The main thrust of the Old Testament is that God is one God. Although there are many references to the Spirit of God (i.e., Isaiah 40.13, Psalm 51.11), and to the Son of God (Psalm 2.7, Isaiah 7.14, Daniel 3.25), the main focus of the Old Testament is on God the Father. It would, however, be fair to say that clarity about God as Father does not come until we get into the New Testament, and then looking back we can see that He is the Father of all mankind (1 Corinthians 8.6) and Father to the nation of Israel (Isaiah 63.16).

In the Gospels, we see the revelation of God in the Son of God. The life of the Lord Jesus is the living revelation of deity to the human heart and mind (John 20.31).

The present stage of the revelation of God to man is the age of the Spirit of God. In John's Gospel chapter 16 verse 7, the Lord tells the disciples that it is to their advantage that He goes away, for "If I go not away, the Comforter will not come unto you; but if I depart, I will send Him unto you" [AV] (The Comforter is another title of the Holy Spirit, see John 14 verses 15-16). Upon the ascension of the Lord Jesus, He sent the Spirit of God into the world, see also John 7.39.

Q.4: What does the Holy Spirit do for a believer today?

One of the best books in the Bible to turn to for the answer to this question is the Epistle of Paul to the Ephesians. This letter is packed full of references to the Spirit of God. All the points raised are very instructive regarding the work of the Holy Spirit in our lives.

The references from Ephesians are given below with a brief highlight of the teaching of each portion:

Ephesians 1.3: The believer has blessings which are spiritual in character as opposed to the natural (material or earth-related) blessings that this world has to offer. This means they are eternal and of infinitely greater value.

Ephesians 1.13, 14: On the day we got saved, we were sealed with that Holy Spirit of promise.

This marked us out as belonging to God (1 Corinthians 6.20) and assured us of future blessing (1 Peter 1.4). The second thing mentioned here is that the Holy Spirit is the 'earnest of our inheritance' [AV]. The word 'earnest' is taken from the commercial world and the world of romance. The idea is of a payment made in advance, as the proof that the purchaser has the ability to complete the deal in the future. It was also used to describe the equivalent of the engagement ring, the purchase of which was seen as the proof that the husband could afford to look after his intended bride. In this context, the Holy Spirit is to the believer the down payment and the evidence that we will one day, on the day of redemption, be joint heirs with Christ.

Ephesians 1.17: Paul prays for the believer's spiritual understanding through the work of the indwelling Spirit of God. The wording is lovely: 'That the God of our Lord Jesus Christ, the Father of glory, may give to you the spirit of wisdom and revelation in the knowledge of Him'. The Spirit of God opens the eyes of believers to give them a deepening awareness of the blessings that they have in the Lord Jesus Christ.

Ephesians 2.18: As a result of the work of Christ, by means of His death on the cross, the Spirit of God is able to bring all believers into the presence of the Father. Note again the work of the Trinity: the price is paid by the Son, and access is given by the Spirit of God, into the presence of the Father.

Ephesians 2.22: Generally, Ephesians is about the church which is the body of Christ as opposed to the local church. In verse 21, Paul has been teaching that the body of Christ is growing into a holy temple for the Lord. This means at the end of the church age, when the Lord Jesus comes, the church will be complete and the Lord Jesus will dwell among His people. Verse 22 adds that the local church is being built together as the dwelling place of God on earth through the Holy Spirit. This is a wonderful truth to remember as we gather as local churches - God is dwelling among His people through the work of the Holy Spirit.

Ephesians 3.5: Everything that we know about God, His character and His way of dealing with us, has been communicated to us through the Holy Spirit. In Ephesians, God is revealing new truth about the gospel, the church and how God includes all of humanity in this blessing. In the Old Testament, God spoke to 'the fathers by the prophets', but when the Lord Jesus came, He spoke 'by His Son' (Hebrews 1.1-2). In the rest of the New Testament, God spoke to the holy apostles and prophets through the Holy Spirit. Peter confirms this when he writes in 2 Peter chapter 1 verse 21 about holy men of God speaking 'as they were moved by the Holy Spirit'.

Ephesians 3.16: Life can be hard, and experiences can be very exhausting for many people. Every believer has, however, access to unlimited resources which God has made available. This verse states in great detail now this works:

   (a) It is free of charge - it has been granted to you.

   (b) It draws from an unlimited resource - it is according to the riches of His glory.

   (c) It directly meets a need - you will be strengthened.

   (d) The Spirit of God who dwells in you brings this strength to you.

   (e) It is spiritual strength - 'in the inner man'.

This final point does not mean that God cannot give you physical strength, but that when physical strength is waning, God can renew and restore your inner man day by day - see 2 Corinthians 4.7-18.

Ephesians 4.3, 4: In human terms, maintaining harmony and unity within any group of people is very demanding. It should be easier among Christians and in a church context, but human nature being what it is, all the same tensions often come to the surface. It is therefore very interesting that Paul makes an appeal to the Ephesian believers to 'walk worthy' and to endeavour to maintain unity. It is also very significant that the apostle teaches that the unity among Christians is not created or enforced by us. The unity exists because the Holy Spirit brought the church into existence on the Day of Pentecost (1 Corinthians 12.13), and we were made part of the church on the day of our conversion (even though in one sense it was in the mind of God long before time began, Ephesians 1.4). It is part of our responsibility as saints to make every effort to preserve this unity which the Holy Spirit has created.

Ephesians 4.30: In this verse, we are reminded that we could grieve the Holy Spirit. The preceding verses specifically warn that lies, anger, stealing, selfishness, foul and abusive language, are all ways in which we could grieve the Holy Spirit. We thought earlier in this chapter about the personal qualities of the Spirit of God. These verses make it very clear that He has feelings and there are things about our behaviour that could upset Him.

Ephesians 5.9: The most famous verses in the Bible about the fruit of the Spirit are found in Galatians chapter 5 verses 22 and 23. It would be worth reading those verses just now. Our verse here has a brief reference to the fruit of the Spirit in a believer's life. Paul reminds his readers that when they were unsaved they were classified as darkness, but now they are 'light in the Lord'. He is describing the world they lived in and how it characterised them. Once they got saved, things changed. They now live in the world of the light, and so as children of light the way they live should reflect this. It is as if Paul gives us three examples of the fruit of the Spirit - goodness, righteousness and truth. Now he says that living like that really pleases the Lord (v.10).

Ephesians 5.18: We learned from chapter 1 verse 13 that at the point of conversion, the believer received the Spirit of God. The emphasis is slightly different in this verse. This isn't about how much of the Spirit we get at salvation, for we learned earlier that the Spirit of God is a person and you can't just have part of a person in your life. The point here is, How much of your life does the Spirit have? Here we are exhorted to be filled with the Spirit, as opposed to being under the influence of alcohol. Are you filled with the Spirit, or do you limit what part the Spirit of God plays in your life? We would need to consult other passages to get an idea of how to go about being filled with the Spirit. It's worth looking into, and vital for healthy Christian living.

Ephesians 6.17: The next reference to the Holy Spirit is found in a section which describes the spiritual body armour that God has made available to every believer (6.10-18). In these verses, the Bible, the Word of God, is described as 'the sword of the Spirit'. Most of the armour is to protect and preserve. There is little in the list that would be used as an offensive weapon, and so the Word of God should be used to protect the believer. It will preserve us from evil (going back) and will assist us in moving forward in the battle. The greatest example of the effective use of the Scriptures against the 'strategies of the devil' (v.11, [NLT]) is seen in how the Lord Jesus confronted Satan when He was tested in the Wilderness (Matthew 4.1-11, Mark 1.12, 13, Luke 4.1-13). He skilfully quotes from Deuteronomy each time He replies to Satan's temptation. We should try to learn how to be skilful in our use of the sword of the Spirit.

Ephesians 6.18: The final reference concludes the teaching about the believer's spiritual body armour by reminding us that the Spirit of God should be involved in our prayer life. Our prayers should be in line with the will of God through the work of the Spirit.

There are many other references in the New Testament to the person and work of the Holy Spirit, all of which are very instructive for the Christian. I have selected these verses from Ephesians to make it easier to follow the train of thought, and because many of them link the work of the Spirit with that of the Father and the Son.

CHAPTER 8

Conclusion

I hope that I have shown you from the Bible that God is a complex Being, and yet He is someone each of us can relate to. We can relate to Him through faith in the Son of God, the Lord Jesus Christ.

It would take a far larger book than this to answer all of the questions that have been raised about the character of God, but one question which people often ask is, Why is God a Trinity?

There is no absolute answer to this question. It's like asking why we have two eyes or ten toes. That's the way God created us.

So why is God the Father, the Son, and the Holy Spirit, all one God, and yet individual and distinctive? The simple answer is - that's the way God is. That is how He has revealed Himself to us so that we could know about Him and relate to Him.

It is important for each of us to know as much as we can *about Him*, and I hope that this book has helped you in this. But it is even more important for us to get to *know Him* for ourselves, as *our* God. Before going to the cross to die, the Lord Jesus prayed to His Father: 'And this is eternal life, *that they might know You*, the only true God, and Jesus Christ whom You have sent' (John 17.3).

To get to know Him as **our** God, we will need to be trusting Him each day, praying for His help and guidance, reading His precious Word, loving Him with all our heart (Matthew 22.37). We will be loving and following His Son, our Lord and Saviour Jesus Christ. The apostle Paul said that his ambition was, 'that I may know Him' (Philippians 3.10). He and many others, called God, '*My* God' (Philippians 4.19). Can you say that too?

The great truth of the Trinity is that it is the perfect expression of the character of God. As we gaze upon the Father, the Son, and the Spirit in all their individual perfections and delightful unity, we get a glimpse of their single and united majesty.

We learn, we get to know Him better, and we can worship Him more intelligently. I pray that this will be your experience each day.

Yours through grace,

Stephen

Bibliography
Appendix 1

Does God believe in Atheists, John Blanchard, Evangelical Press

Seven reasons why you can trust the Bible, Erwin W. Lutzer, Moody Bible Institute

God Breathed, Josh McDowell

The Undeniable Power and Reliability of Scripture, Shiloh Run Press, An Imprint of Barbour Publishing, Inc

The New Evidence That Demands a Verdict, Josh McDowell, Nashville: Thomas Nelson, 1999

Ring of Truth, J B Phillips, *A Translator's Testimony,* Hodder & Stoughton

Are the New Testament Documents Reliable? F F Bruce, The Inter-Varsity Fellowship

The Holy Trinity, H A Ironside, CrossReach Publications

The Trinity and the Bible, Scott R. Swain, Lexham Academic

Making Sense of the Trinity, Millard J. Erickson, Baker Academic

BIBLIOGRAPHY

Please note that acknowledging that I consulted these books does not mean that I agreed with all that the authors taught about the Trinity or other biblical issues, but that they stimulated me to explore further what the Scriptures teach on the topic.

Acknowledgements
Appendix 2

The idea for this book came about because of requests from believers in Pakistan for a simple outline explanation of the character of God with a clear emphasis on the truth of the Trinity as presented in Scripture. God is more majestic and complex than any one individual could ever explain. This book is an attempt to highlight the key Scriptures that address the topic. I am very aware that many have preached on these truths and others have written detailed and informative books on the subject. I have benefitted from their ministry.

A short book like this would not be possible without the input of many people. I would like to thank Bert Cargill for editing and proofreading the manuscript along with Fraser Munro. Their meticulous and careful attention to detail is invaluable.

Finally, thank you for reading this book. Without a readership there is no reason to write books. I couldn't have done it without you.